POETRY

VOLUME ONE

POETRY

VOLUME ONE

MARK LITTLE

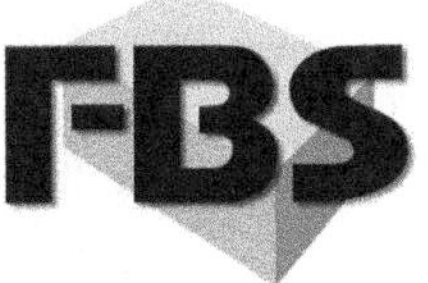

FABULOUSBOOKS
www.fbs-publishing.co.uk

First Published in the UK September 2017 by FBS Publishing Ltd.
22 Dereham Road, Thetford,
Norfolk. IP25 6ER
ISBN 978-0-9932043-8-8

A CIP catalogue record for this book is
available from the British Library.

Cover and illustrations by Mark Little
Text Edited by Alasdair McKenzie
Typesetting and Graphics by John Ainsworth

Paper stock used is natural, recyclable and made from wood grown in sustainable forests. The manufacturing processes conform to environmental regulations.

To Cathy X

EXISTENCE

She Sat Across From Me

She sat across from me,
Silently,
Scared.
Amid a sea of white,
That doesn't seem,
To care.
She sat across from me,
Silently,
Scared.
Alert to every nuance.
Impressively.
Aware.
She sat across from me,
Silently,
Scared.
Not once our eyes did meet,
As if she did not dare,
She sat across from me,
Silently,

Scared.
Invoked in me a desperate need
For something to be shared.
A careful look, a smile.
Even tears or howling rage.
But she sat across from me,
Silently,
Scared.
A young and beautiful Aussie.
Aboriginal.
I longed to stand and cry out.
What a mess.
I am so sorry.
But
I did not dare.
I just sat across from her,
Silently,
Scared!

Tent Five Oh Six

He sat in tent 506
Stewin' in his own psychotics.
Day and Night and Day he sat,
Just staring out ... Just like that.
Igloo style—very small tent,
Emotions bubbling repression pent.
Roll up! Roll up! Forget the mirth,
See the saddest man on Earth.
Under the Little Top, a one man
show!
He's gunna crack! he's gunna blow!
He sat in tent Five Oh Six.
Stewin' in his own psychotics!

AM I DREAMING

THE ROCKS ARE ORANGE! AND PURPLE!
INDIGO! GREEN! AND GREY!
THE SKY A DEEP AZURE!
MOST BLUE IN EVERY WAY!
THE SAND ELECTRIC BEIGE!
THE TREE TRUNKS, SNOW-BLIND WHITE
AND THE FLIES?
YOU GUESSED IT!
IRIDESCENT AQUAMARINE!!
THE LEAVES ARE CUTLERY SILVER!
THE DRAGON FLIES QUITE TRANSPARENTLY.
TWO CROWS GLIDE PAST, OUT OF THE SUN,
POLISHED METAL,
BLACK ALUMINIUM,
APPARENTLY!
IT'S BEEN THIS WAY
FOR THOUSANDS OF YEARS
THE ORIGINALS CALL IT DREAMING.
SO, IN THE AUSSIE DESERT
I SIT.
TUNED IN!
CUT OFF!
AND WONDER!
AM I DREAMING?
I HOPE SO!
2006

Dog Gone (Poem for a Dead Dingo)

Goodbye Dingo you Drongo,
Your time as a dog
Has gone.
A life of eating
And creating Pedigree Dung.
A life of greeting
And barking and
Guarding and sleep.
You gave us all your
Love Dingo,
For little in return.
Hello Ding!
Good dog Ding!
Well done Ding!
So we lay you in the hole
You loved.
Much better than shovin'
You in an urn.
So goodbye Dingo,
We loved you pretty much.
We loved you like a dog.
Now run off into the afterlife
And I hope you find
Your God.
Good Girl!!!

2017 Any IDEAS?

Any ideas?
To allay my fears?
To dam my tears?
Any ideas?
Any thoughts?
I'm out of sorts?
Is it all for nought?
Any thoughts?
Any Love?
Have you got it?
Can you bring it?
Any Love?
Any Ideas?
Any Thoughts?
Any Love?
Only Fear?

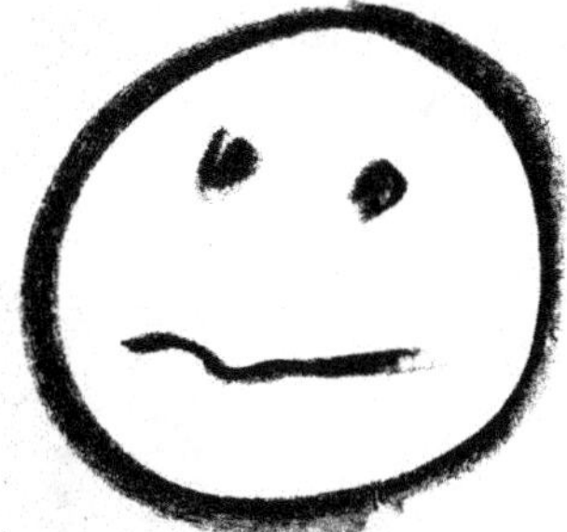

Available Clown

'How funny can you be?'
I asked the available clown.
'How funny do you wish?'
Answered the available clown with a frown.
'What ya got?'
'Not a lot.'
'Should we leave it there then?'
'I think so. There'll be another clown along in a couple of minutes.'
And that's how I learned not to expect too much from the Available Clown.

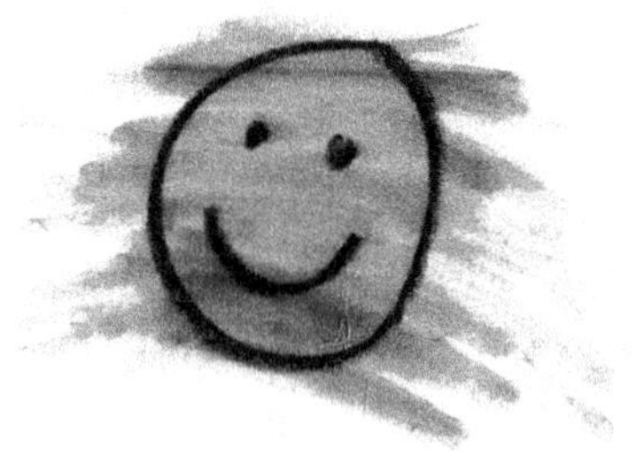

In the Garden of Despair

In the garden of despair,
Where …
The vines of apathy strangle,
Creeping, cynicism tangled.
Hope withers. Choked of Air.

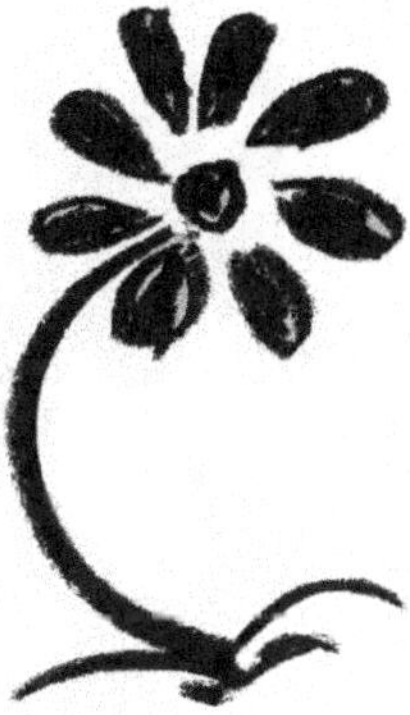

And yet, in the 'garden of gloom'
Amid the Overgrown Doom,
There smiles a flower,
The flower of you.
With the smiling flower of you,
Seeing you,
Hearing you,
My love peeks out.
You lift my heart.
I weep at your beauty,
From the midst of a mire of drudge,
You lift my heart.
You are my flower.
My love.
My smile.
And I will always love you.
Thank you for being my flower
In 'the dark garden' of my life.
Thank you for your smiling love.
If it wasn't for you, I'd never get in the garden at all.
I will always love you.
2015

Inert

Inert
Stopped
Stalled
Stagnant
Rotting
Fix it!

Love

To You Rimbaud

Sweet beast
Of youth,
Soft and
Violent heart.
Crucify him!
Remember him!
Savage Poet
Dead to the charms
Of destruction.
Too much life
For one pen!
To Hell
And back,
Raped
By words, thoughts, deeds, dreams.
Nightmares.
Thence?
Piss on everything.
Defy them.
Rewrite them.
Damn them all
To the world of the poet
To Hell …
… To you!

2012

<u>My Little Pearl</u>

I love you,
I really do.
I Rage at what they did to you!
My little girl,
My little pearl.
Prised too early from your shell
To start your life in someone's hell!
It's a cruel world.
My little pearl,
I love you,
My little girl.
I Really do,
My little pearl!
I want to clasp you in my palms!
Take you softly in my arms!
And kiss you very fondly till!
You are very much better well!

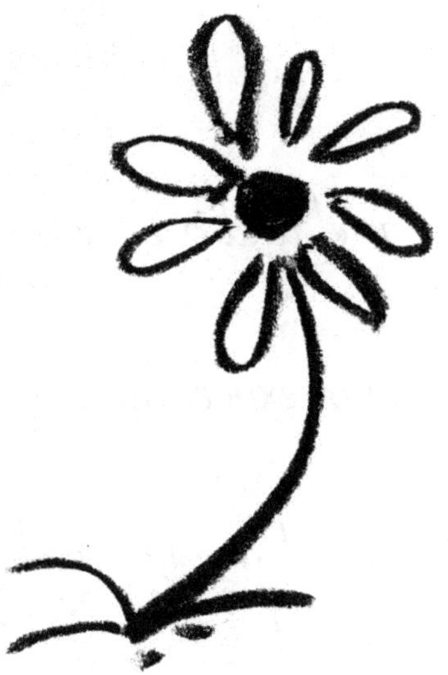

SORRY YOU ARE THERE

I miss you in your sorrow,

I miss you in your grief.

Sorry I can't be with you,

Such is life, I believe.

It's a long, horrible journey,

To grief and beyond,

I'm not expecting a postcard,

Really. Hope you're home safe
and sound.

Your friend was so near, you hold him
so dear.

You've cried an ocean for his loneliness
and all that fear.

You are in a place you should not be. Come home
safe. My quiet plea.

My love is with you, while you
are there.

Remember,

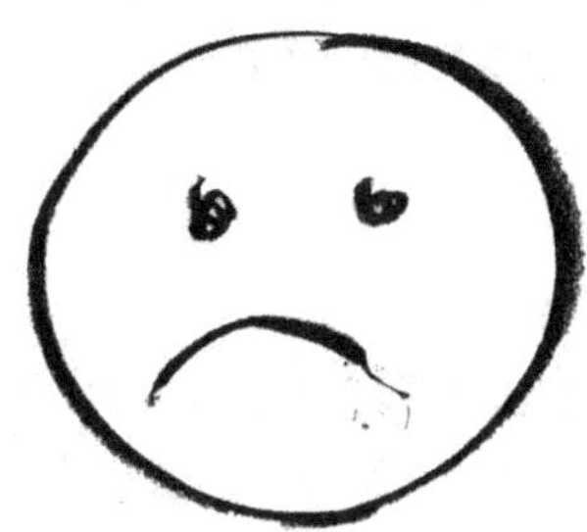

You will always return, for

Forever is a long time to visit.

As a flower pressed.
Stressed.
Pressure Absorbed.
Beauteous.
So you are my sweetest.
Pressed.
Stressed.
Pressure Absorbed.
Beauteous.
Never to Wilt.
Happy Love. My love,
It is late. I know.
Dearest Love. My love,
It has been another poor show!
I've been a cad
And a villain.
A misfit
Unforgiven.
A Bounder. A Loser.
As old as Methuselah.
A Wrong'n, a Brute,
A right Bobby Dazzler,
A Nong and a Beast
And A Dill at very Least

PERFORMANCE

#secretmeeting

Here I stand, stood on a box,
Startled like an urban fox.
I live in London but not in fear,
But there is a strange atmosphere.

Planet Earth lives in fear.
Jihadis, Jihadis everywhere.
Anti-Muslim, Anti-Jew,
Foodbanks too.

And Billionaires,
Climate Change
Tory Mayors.
There's Fracking of course,

That's going to hurt.
Droning countries back to dirt
Celebrity Paedos,
Celebrity Peers.

Can you tell what it is yet?
For years and years and years …

Austerity, theft.
NHS. Stolen.
Humanity, bereft.
Bankers' wallets swollen.

But this is just a poem;

Don't let it get you down,
The answer is quite simple,
We have to smash them down.

Smash down those Tory bigots,
Those UKIP Nazis too,
Throw something heavy at them,
Something heavy, like your shoe.

For we are smart enough
As the fools conspire against us,
And we must stand up
And cry out

Fuck off you idiots
We are not afraid.
You are all corrupt
And highly overpaid.

2015: Performed at *Mark Little's #SECRETMEETINGS*

Angry Nude

Here I stand, Angry and Nude
Not to be rude
Nor crude
Nor Lewd
I stand before you
Angry and Nude
To rail against the media gods
Teasing us with semi-nude frustrations
Commercial false alarms of
Sexual liberations
Angry and nude
The media makes us sick
When it comes to this subject
I have a very short wick

Performed nude in *Spontaneous Human Combustion*
1998

BRIT POP

It's a funny old summer
It's a bit of a bummer
The rain keeps a fallin' …
A shame I am callin' …
It!

Didn't win footy
Gettin' sick of Sooty
Glastonbury was muddy
Hooligans are bloody …
Thick!

Television is shit
Radio just a bit
Life is unfortunate
So disproportion …
ate!

Cool Britannia
Oasis mania
It's called New Labour
It's the flava …
of the month!

The song is nearly gone
Thank Christ, it went on and on
But let's have a sing-a-long
I am a whingeing Pom

I am a whingeing Pom
I am a whingeing Pom
I am a whingeing Pom
I am a whingeing Pom

Sung in *Spontaneous Human Combustion* 1998

Fascists on the Moon

Soon we'll live in space
In space, we'll live real soon
But we'll have to find another place
Cause there's fascists on the moon
fascists on the moon
fascists on the moon

Fascists on the telly
Fascists on the bus
Fascists fundamentally
Are not like us

Fascists don't like thinking
Not that very much
A fascist without blinking
Will leave you in the dust

Soon we'll live in space
In space we'll live real soon
But we'll have to find another place
Because there's fascists on the moon
fascists on the moon
fascists on the moon

Fascism is crazy
Fascists drive us mad
Fascism's not lazy
And it's very, very sad

Fascism is creeping
Fascism is now
The people have been sleeping
But it’s time to wake up now

Soon we’ll live in space
In space we’ll live real soon
But we’ll have to find another place
Because there’s fascists on the moon
fascists on the moon
fascists on the moon (repeat forever)

Recorded for *The Acid Punch* 2017

A Message to Space

**I sent a message to Google Earth,
I sent a message to Space.
I sent a message to Google Earth,
It was very in your face.
'Fuck Off' it said,
In bold white letters.
'Fuck Off' it plainly read.
I sent a message to Google Earth,
It washed off in the night.
A message all the way to space,
The rain washed it off … one night!
I'll have to send again,
My message to Google Earth.
I'll have to send again,
My message into Space.
And what will it say,
This message to space?
'Fuck Off' of course, what else!
'Fuck Off' out of my face.**

2017 *The Acid Punch*

Damien Hirst 1995

Damien Hirst,
Has a particular thirst,
For the offensive
And the macabre.
From a 20-foot shark
To half a cow and
Its calf
Is it Art?
Is it Art?
Is it Art?
Damien Hirst,
Most probably first,
To see the beauty of maggot.
But Damien Hirst,
Don't expect me to burst,
Till you whack that formaldehyde
In Taggart.

Politik

DOOM

For Whom the Doom Looms
KABOOM
Goes the Room
Vaporize the Groom
No need for a Broom
As the Doom Looms
KABOOM
MUTANT WOMB
TOXIC BLOOM
RADIOACTIVE TOMB
Smiling Politicians
Saturday Sunday
Doomsday
A Very Long Weekend
The End
Is Nigh, if we don't try
To stop Atomic Dickheads
For, 'Tis us For Whom the
Doom Looms,
KABOOM.

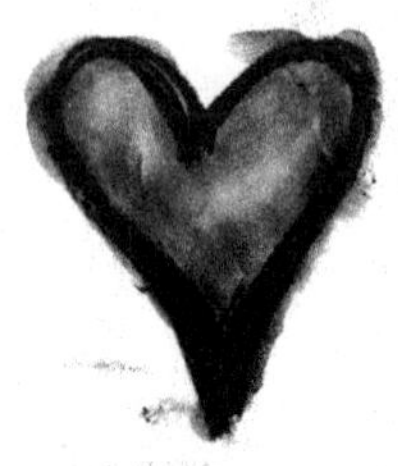

#Paris

**It's easy-breezy, sleazy,
In the City of Love.
It's hot, coffee, hot,
In the City of Love.
Life on the streets,
In the City of Love.
Mad, sad and dangerous,
In the City of Love.
Now poisoned politics,
In the City of Love.
Bullets raining down,
In the City of Love.
Terrorist fear,
In the City of Love.
Too many dead,
In the City of Love.
Everyone's consumed,
In the City of Love.
Love underground,
In the City of Love.
Deep underground,
In the City of Love.**

Rise Up

I am the oppressed,
Angry and Tired.
In a metaphysical cage.
Beaten with lies.
Time to escape.
Revitalise.
Think.
Act.
Take Over!
Rise! Rise!! Rise!!!

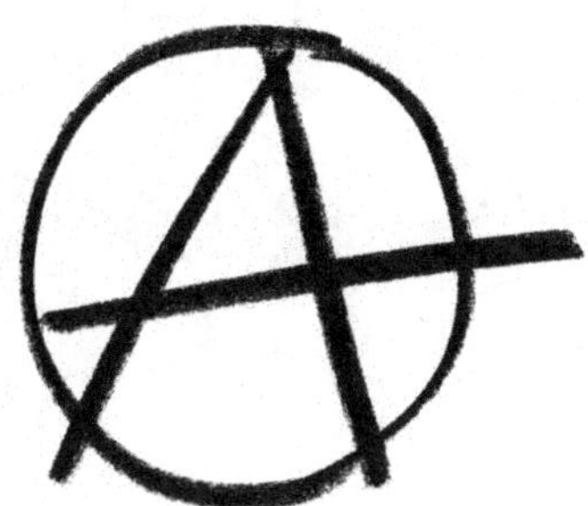

About the Author

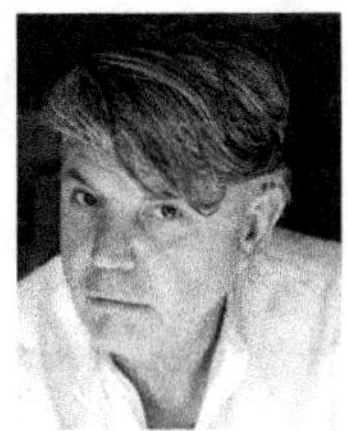

Mark Little was born in Brisbane, Australia and spent his childhood in rural Queensland. He trained as an actor at the National Institute of Dramatic Art in Sydney.

Mark is best known for his portrayal of Joe Mangel in the soap phenomenon *Neighbours* where he created one of Ramsay Street's legendary characters. He had previously played Ron Miller in *The Flying Doctors* and was presented with the Australian Television Society Award for Best Actor. In the UK, he has appeared in several television dramas including the BBC's *Casualty* and the ITV soap *Emmerdale*.

He has starred in sixteen feature films and written and performed numerous live comedy shows at the Edinburgh Fringe. He also appeared in the West End receiving and Olivier Award for *Defending the Caveman*. Mark is fondly remembered for being a presenter on Channel 4's *The Big Breakfast*. He is now a regular panelist on *The Wright Stuff* for Channel 5.

He is currently writing, performing and directing his series on YouTube entitled *The Acid Punch*, a creative collaboration with Ohh Mamma Films. This book is his first volume of poetry.

www.markedmundlittle.co.uk

Follow Mark on Twitter @themarklittle

WRITE OWN POEM

↓ HERE ↓

Tweet your poem to @FBSPublishing #POETRY ♥

www.ingramcontent.com/pod-product-compliance
Lightning Source LLC
La Vergne TN
LVHW010841120826
845149LV00020B/3487

* 9 7 8 0 9 9 3 2 0 4 3 8 8 *